SOUTH AMERICA

XINA M. UHL

Rourke
Educational Media

rourkeeducationalmedia.com

Before & After Reading Activities

Before Reading:

Building Academic Vocabulary and Background Knowledge

Before reading a book, it is important to tap into what your child or students already know about the topic. This will help them develop their vocabulary, increase their reading comprehension, and make connections across the curriculum.

1. *Look at the cover of the book. What will this book be about?*
2. *What do you already know about the topic?*
3. *Let's study the Table of Contents. What will you learn about in the book's chapters?*
4. *What would you like to learn about this topic? Do you think you might learn about it from this book? Why or why not?*
5. *Use a reading journal to write about your knowledge of this topic. Record what you already know about the topic and what you hope to learn about the topic.*
6. *Read the book.*
7. *In your reading journal, record what you learned about the topic and your response to the book.*
8. *After reading the book complete the activities below.*

Content Area Vocabulary
Read the list. What do these words mean?

democracy
developed
dictators
economy
equator
ethnic groups
export
gauchos
isthmus
nomads

After Reading:

Comprehension and Extension Activity

After reading the book, work on the following questions with your child or students in order to check their level of reading comprehension and content mastery.
1. Why did South American plants and animals develop the way they did? (Infer)
2. How did South America's people change over time? (Summarize)
3. What sort of governments did the Spanish and Portuguese conquerors establish? (Asking Questions)
4. How is family life in South America the same as yours? How is it different? (Text to Self Connection)
5. What sort of lives do South America's poor have? (Asking Questions)

Extension Activity

Pick one of South America's countries. Research that country's natural resources on the Internet or using books in your local library. How do people use these resources? How are they related to the country's economy? Write a paragraph that answers these questions. Then, draw a map of the country and pinpoint its natural resources using icons that represent each one.

TABLE OF CONTENTS

Countries in South America:
- Argentina
- Bolivia
- Brazil
- Chile
- Colombia
- Ecuador
- Guyana
- Paraguay
- Peru
- Suriname
- Uruguay
- Venezuela

CONTINENT AND COUNTRIES

The continent of South America is unique and diverse. River basins feed thick rainforests and soggy marshes. Mountain peaks climb high into the sky and grasses make up flat prairies. Hot, dry deserts spread in long strips of land.

Shaped like a triangle, South America is nearly twice the size of the United States. A narrow strip of land, the Isthmus of Panama, connects it with North America.

Except for the **isthmus**, the Atlantic and Pacific Oceans surround it.

North and South America were named after Amerigo Vespucci, an Italian explorer.

The **equator** stretches across the north. The sun shines hot, and makes the days each 12 hours long year-round. Moist, green forests cover the area. Tall, cold mountain peaks run along the western coast in a long range. Deserts and grasslands have a milder climate. The south is cool and dry.

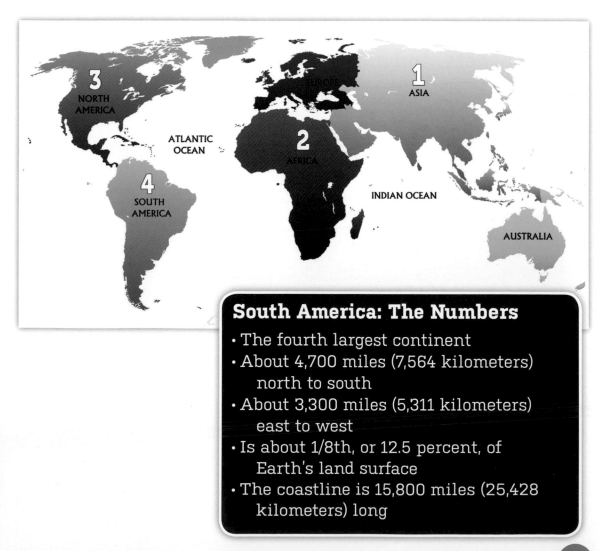

South America: The Numbers

- The fourth largest continent
- About 4,700 miles (7,564 kilometers) north to south
- About 3,300 miles (5,311 kilometers) east to west
- Is about 1/8th, or 12.5 percent, of Earth's land surface
- The coastline is 15,800 miles (25,428 kilometers) long

THE LAND

South America holds many records. The Andes are the longest mountain range in the world. It runs down the western side for about 5,500 miles (8,900 kilometers). The Amazon basin holds the world's biggest rainforest at 2,300,000 square miles (6,000,000 square kilometers). Millions of plants, birds, insects, and animals live there.

The Amazon River is thought to carry about one-sixth of the world's fresh water.

The Amazon River is the second longest in the world. It stretches across the land for about 4,000 miles (6,400 kilometers). In Venezuela flows Angel Falls, the world's tallest waterfall at 3,280 feet (1,000 meters).

Ushuaia is the southernmost city in the world. It's part of a group of islands in Argentina called Tierra del Fuego.

Plants grow abundantly. Cattle and sheep graze on thick grasses in the Pampas region in Argentina. The Amazon basin supports many trees, such as palms, hardwoods, and rubber trees. Llamas, alpacas, guanacos, and capybaras are examples of native wildlife.

South America's natural resources form the basis of its **economy**.

South America's natural resources contain great reserves of iron and copper. Coffee and cacao are important crops.

THE PAST

The **nomads** who became American Indians moved into South America 10,000 to 15,000 years ago. Thousands of years later they settled down to grow crops and build cities. Over time, civilizations came and went.

The ruins of Machu Picchu were unknown until a local resident led a Yale University professor to them in 1911.

The Inca Empire rose in the 1400s, holding land from Ecuador to Chile. Near their capital in Cuzco, Peru, stands the mountain peak called Machu Picchu. It looms 7,710 feet (2,350 meters) tall, and includes great temples, plazas, and terraces.

Statue of Francisco Pizarro

In the late 1400s, Europeans began searching for new trade routes. Pedro Álvares Cabral discovered South America in 1500. He and other explorers learned of the Inca's great riches. In 1532, Francisco Pizarro sailed from Spain with a small army. He and his men conquered the Inca. From there, they went on to conquer many other tribes. Indian tribes often fought back. Still, many of them died from European diseases. No one knows how many died, but the number is in the millions.

The Spanish and Portuguese also took Indians as slaves. Europeans needed more labor for large farms called plantations. In Brazil, sugarcane farms required lots of workers. To meet this need, Europeans imported up to 2.5 million African slaves. Slaves lived hard lives working in mines or on farms. When they could, they ran away. Over time, slavery ended.

Simón Bolívar is known by the Spanish term El Libertador, which means "The Liberator."

In the 1800s, Simón Bolívar fought to end foreign rule. He and his allies brought independence to Venezuela, Colombia, Panama, Ecuador, Peru, and Bolivia. Brazil threw off Portuguese rule in 1822.

These republics called themselves free. In the 20th century, the use of rubber in car tires caused a boom in rubber tree farming. The growth of these farms brought about 100,000 people to Brazil.

Latex, made up of about 30 percent rubber, oozes from holes in rubber tree bark.

American Indians, Africans, and Europeans are South America's main **ethnic groups**. Mestizos are people of mixed races, mostly American Indians and Europeans.

PEOPLE'S LIVES

About 400 million people live in South America. Half of them live in Brazil. They speak Portuguese. Most of the other half live within 200 miles (322 kilometers) of the coast. They speak Spanish.

So many people have moved to cities that they have grown quite large. An example is São Paulo, Brazil, with more than 21 million people. Buenos Aires, Argentina, has 15 million people and Rio de Janeiro, Brazil, has 13 million. Slums called favelas have sprung up around them.

Christianity is the most popular religion. Most South Americans are Roman Catholic Christians.

People and Language in South America		
Country	Population	Official Languages
Argentina	44,293,293	Spanish
Bolivia	11,138,234	Spanish; Native Languages (Quechua, Aymara, Guarani)
Brazil	207,353,391	Portuguese
Chile	17,789,267	Spanish
Colombia	47,698,524	Spanish
Ecuador	16,290,913	Spanish
Peru	243,000	French
Guyana	737,718	English
Paraguay	6,943,739	Spanish; Guarani
Suriname	591,919	Dutch
Uruguay	3,360,148	Spanish
Venezuela	31,304,016	Spanish

Cairo, Egypt, is the largest desert city in the world, followed by Lima, Peru.

Democracy, at least in part, is the foundation of many South American governments. They hold regular elections. But this has not always been the case. Many governments have been overthrown. In such cases, the military or small groups of the rich take charge. They ignore the will of the

Nicolás Maduro became the president of Venezuela in 2013. He has been labeled a dictator by the U.S government.

people. These rulers take power over the laws, courts, and police. **Dictators** rise up in some places. They usually abuse their power. Bad rulers often lose power. The new governments that take their place may not be much better.

Corruption plagues the legal systems. Prisons can be filthy and filled with disease. Police often take bribes. Though there are few rich people, they hold much of the continent's wealth. Huge divides exist between rich and poor. Poverty and crime are high. The poorest countries are Bolivia, Paraguay, Suriname, and Guyana. Chile, Brazil, and Argentina are the richest. Even the richest countries struggle with poverty.

Poor and rich areas of Rio de Janeiro.

19

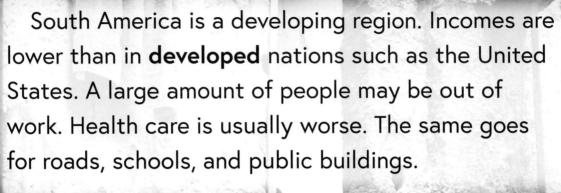

South America is a developing region. Incomes are lower than in **developed** nations such as the United States. A large amount of people may be out of work. Health care is usually worse. The same goes for roads, schools, and public buildings.

Jobs vary depending on the region's resources. **Gauchos** herd cattle in Argentina, Uruguay, and Brazil. Farmers tend fields of coffee beans in Colombia and Brazil. Cacao crops grow in Peru, Ecuador, and Brazil. Miners extract minerals and petroleum in various places. Anchovies, salmon, and shrimp make up the biggest fishing industries. The **export** of illegal drugs like cocaine is big business, too. The prices of these products rise and fall. This has made it hard for countries to build up other markets to support their **economies**.

Organizations called cartels produce hundreds of millions of dollars in illegal drugs every year.

CUSTOMS AND CULTURES

Daily life consists of work or school, and family time. Families include aunts, uncles, cousins, and close friends as well as parents and children. Most countries have large public school systems. The poor often do not finish high school.

Holidays are important events. Ten countries celebrate independence days in July, August, and September. Religion inspires holidays such as All Souls' Day in November. In Rio de Janeiro, Carnival is held 40 days before Easter. This holiday attracts millions who decorate floats, watch parades, and dress in elaborate costumes.

RECIPE: FEIJOADA

Lunch on Wednesdays and Sundays are the traditional times for Brazil's national dish. This large meal serves six people.

Ingredients:

1 pound, 2 ounces (500 grams) dried black beans

14 ounces (400 grams) dried salted meat, cut into small pieces

7 ounces (200 grams) each, diced: bacon, smoked chorizo, calabresa sausage, black pudding sausage, smoked pork belly, and pork legs

1 pound 2 ounces (500 grams) pork ribs smoked

3 bay leaves

2 garlic cloves, chopped

1 onion, finely chopped

2 tablespoons (30 milliliters) parsley, chopped

1 bird's eye chili pepper, chopped

1 tablespoon (15 milliliters) salt

1 teaspoon (5 milliliters) ground black pepper

Directions:

1. Place beans in a pot to soak in water. Add dried salted meat. Change water at least four times every three hours.

2. Add half of the rest of the meat to the pot along with 34 ounces (1 liter) of water and bay leaves. Bring to a boil. Reduce the heat, cover, and simmer for 1.5 hours.

3. Mix in the rest of the meat except for the bacon. Cook for 1.5 more hours.

4. Heat vegetable oil in a skillet. Cook bacon, onion, garlic, parsley and chili for 10 minutes. Mash some cooked black beans to create a thick sauce. Add salt and pepper. Combine with beans and meat.

5. Simmer for 15 minutes.

6. Serve with orange segments, cooked white rice, and steamed broccoli or kale.

Soccer is the most popular sport in South America. Dance parties are held often, too. The quick-moving tango comes from Argentina. Dancers sometimes practice it in the streets.

African slaves were said to use capoeira in order to escape capture. Capoeira became illegal after 1888, when slavery ended in Brazil. After about 40 years it became legal.

Capoeira comes from Africans living in Brazil. This popular art form combines dance, fighting, and movement.

DANCE THE TANGO

Learn to dance the tango alone first, then look for a partner once you know the basics.

Steps:

1. Find tango music on YouTube, your local library, or at school.

2. Imagine you stand opposite a partner. If you are the leading partner, raise your left hand in the air. Place your right arm where your partner's back would be. The following partner holds his or her right hand on the other person's neck. The left hand is on their partner's hip.

In Buenos Aires, tango dancing events may go all night long, ending at 5 or 6 a.m.

3. Be sure to keep your head high. Hold your spine straight, and lift your chest. Show confidence!

4. Practice in this order: slow, slow, quick, quick, slow.

5. Leading partner takes five steps:
   - Left foot forward
   - Right foot forward
   - Left foot forward
   - Move to the right with right foot
   - Bring feet together. Move left to meet your right foot.
   - Repeat

6. Following partner's five steps:
   - Right foot backward
   - Left foot backward
   - Right foot backward
   - Move left with left foot
   - Bring feet together. Move right to meet your left foot.
   - Repeat

7. Now you are ready to add more moves.

GLOSSARY

democracy (di-MOK-ruh-see): a way of governing a country in which the people choose their leaders in elections

developed (di-VEL-uhpt): built on something, or made to grow

dictators (DIK-tay-turz): people who have complete control of a country, often ruling it unjustly

economies (i-KON-uh-meez): the way countries run their industry, trade, and finance

equator (i-KWAY-tur): an imaginary line around the middle of the Earth, halfway between the North and South Poles

ethnic groups (ETH-nik groops): to do with a number of people sharing the same national origins, languages, or cultures

export (ek-SPORT or EK-sport): to send products to another country to be sold there

gauchos (gow-CHOZ): cowboys who works on the Pampas of South America

isthmus (ISS-muhss): a narrow strip of land that lies between two bodies of water and connects two larger land masses

nomads (NOH-madz): a tribe of people that wanders around instead of living in one place

INDEX

SHOW WHAT YOU KNOW

1. What is the South American region around the equator like?

2. What is special about the Amazon Basin?

3. Why did the Spanish conquer the Inca Empire?

4. How is life in South America's developing nations different from developed nations such as the United States?

5. Study the table "People and Languages in South America." Which language do most people in South America speak: Spanish or Portuguese?

FURTHER READING

Randolph, Joanne, *Number Crunch Your Way Around South America*, Rosen Publishing, 2016.

Roberts, Jack L., *A Kid's Guide to South America*, Curious Kids Press, 2017.

Roumanis, Alexis, *South America*, Weigl Publishers Inc., 2015.

ABOUT THE AUTHOR

Xina M. Uhl has written more than twenty educational books for young people, on everything from history to health. She loves to travel, and hopes one day to visit many South American countries.

Meet The Author!
www.meetREMauthors.com

www.rourkeeducationalmedia.com

PHOTO CREDITS: Cover & Title Pg ©rmnunes, ©davidionut, ©Probuxtor, ©By Kotin, ©hadynyah, ©By Maxisport, Top Pg Bar ©fergregory, Pg 3 ©Discovod | Dreamstime.com, Pg 4 ©Boggy | Dreamstime.com, ©Paulliversagephotography | Dreamstime. com, Pg 5 ©Michello | Dreamstime.com, Pg 6 ©Wastesoul | Dreamstime.com, Pg 7 ©Lorenzot81 | Dreamstime.com, ©Alice Nerr, Pg 8 ©Dr Morley Read, Pg 9 ©sunsinger, Pg 10 ©Sjors737 | Dreamstime.com, Pg 10 ©Sjors737 | Dreamstime.com, Pg 11 ©Vitmark | Dreamstime.com, Pg 12 ©By Jose Ignacio Soto, Pg 13 ©De Luan/Alamy Stock Photo, Pg 14 © By Janusz Pienkowski, Pg 15 ©Alffoto | Dreamstime.com, ©By Anton_Ivanov, Pg 16 ©Byvalet | Dreamstime.com, Pg 18 ©By Marcos Salgado, Pg 19 ©Cesar Okada, Pg 20 ©By Elena Odareeva, Pg 21 ©By Couperfield, Pg 22 ©By Ruslana Iurchenko, Pg 23 ©By CP DC Press, Pg 24 ©By rocharibeiro, Pg 25 ©By YARUNIV Studio, Pg 26 ©Amp, Pg 27 ©By Filipe Frazao Pg 28 ©By gary yim, Pg 29 ©By Kaspars Grinvalds

Edited by: Keli Sipperley
Cover design by: Rhea Magaro-Wallace
Interior design by: Corey Mills

Library of Congress PCN Data

South America / Xina M. Uhl
(Earth's Continents)
ISBN 978-1-64156-410-6 (hard cover)
ISBN 978-1-64156-536-3 (soft cover)
ISBN 978-1-64156-660-5 (e-Book)
Library of Congress Control Number: 2018930431

Rourke Educational Media
Printed in the United States of America,
North Mankato, Minnesota